In the last 90 years the extent and pace of change has been truly remarkable. We have witnessed triumphs and tragedies. Our world has enjoyed great advances in science and technology, but it has also endured war, conflict and terrible suffering on an unprecedented scale.

I am touched that Bible Society, HOPE and the London Institute for Contemporary Christianity have published this book to celebrate my 90th birthday. In my first Christmas Broadcast in 1952, I asked the people of the Commonwealth and Empire to pray for me as I prepared to dedicate myself to their service at my Coronation. I have been – and remain – very grateful to you for your prayers and to God for His steadfast love. I have indeed seen His faithfulness.

As I embark on my 91st year, I invite you to join me in reflecting on the words of a poem quoted by my father, King George VI, in his Christmas Day broadcast in 1939, the year that this country went to war for the second time in a quarter of a century.

I said to the man who stood at the Gate of the Year

"Give me a light that I may tread safely into the unknown."

And he replied, "Go out into the darkness, and put your hand into the hand of God.

That shall be to you better than light, and safer than a known way."

ELIZABETH R.

The Servant Queen

written by
**Mark Greene &
Catherine Butcher**

Two things stand out – the Queen's constant sense of duty and her devotion to God. Of this she speaks humbly but openly, especially in her Christmas broadcasts.

William Shawcross,
Royal biographer

1 The Queen's Secret

The Queen is by any measure a remarkable woman.

She's the longest reigning monarch in British history.

She never went to university, but she has been the adviser and confidante to twelve British Prime Ministers.

She's a 90-year-old senior citizen, but still works over 40 hours a week.

She employs 1200 people, but feeds her own dogs.

She can rebuild the 6-cylinder, 3462 cc engine of an Austin K2 Ambulance, trek hatless for hours on her Fell pony across the windswept Highland moors, but she looks entirely comfortable and elegant in the 488 diamond Kokoshnik tiara.

She is the most famous woman in the world, but seems as relaxed in a school, a residential care home or a technology company as in the company of celebrities or other Heads of State.

She is the Supreme Governor of the Church of England, attends church weekly, even on holiday, and prays daily but never tells anyone to go to church.

She has no power to make political decisions but her personal authority has brought nations together.

She has had a gruelling travel and work schedule for over 60 years but as political commentator Andrew Marr pointed out:

> There are no reliable recorded incidents of the Queen losing her temper, using bad language, or refusing to carry out a duty expected of her.

Most of us would find it hard to match that record for a week never mind 60 years.

What is the secret of the Queen's remarkable consistency of character and extraordinary contribution to nation, Commonwealth and the global community?

It's a question she herself answered in 2002.

> I know just how much I rely on my faith to guide me through the good times and the bad. Each day is a new beginning. I know that the only way to live my life is to try to do what is right, to take the long view, to give of my best in all that the day brings, and to put my trust in God ... I draw strength from the message of hope in the Christian gospel.

Many commentators have noted the depth of her trust in God but few have explored it.

We've found it inspiring and hope you do too.

As a Girl Guide Princess Elizabeth promised 'I will do my best to do my duty to God and the King'.

2 The King's Speech & the Princess' Piece

It is December 1939.

Britain has been at war with Germany for three months and no one is under any illusion that what lies ahead will be anything but brutal, heart-wrenching and tragic. On Christmas Day, King George VI, Elizabeth's father, is to speak to nation and Commonwealth. This broadcast will turn out to be even more significant than the address he gave on the outbreak of war that featured in the film, *The King's Speech*.

What do you say to a nation that still bears the scars of the First World War in which more than nine million British and Commonwealth soldiers had died? What do you say when you know that what lies ahead is the loss of sons and husbands and brothers; devastation, privation, terrible suffering? You cannot promise that their loved ones will be protected or that they themselves will be spared.

At the time Elizabeth was 13 years old and the family was still living in Buckingham Palace. She handed her father a poem by Minnie Louise Haskins that she thought might be helpful. She was right. It is indicative of the Queen's self-effacing modesty that she does not mention that fact in her foreword to this book. What mattered then, and still matters to her now, is how the words helped others. And indeed, it was the lines from that poem that stirred and strengthened the hearts of millions at that terrible time:

I said to the man who stood at
the Gate of the Year

'Give me a light that I may tread
safely into the unknown.'

And he replied,

St Paul's Cathedral, London, during the Blitz, 29 December 1940.

'Go out into the darkness, and put your hand into the hand of God.

That shall be to you better than light, and safer than a known way.'

It was a call to the same simple trust in God that has marked her own life – whatever has come.

The Queen is a woman who has looked in two directions for almost her entire life – upwards towards God, and outwards towards her people. It began early and was expressed with such sincerity in her Coronation vows and in her 21st birthday radio address:

> I declare before you all that my whole life whether it be long or short shall be devoted to your service and the service of our great imperial family to which we all belong.
>
> But I shall not have strength to carry out this resolution alone unless you join in it with me, as I now invite you to do: I know that your support will be unfailingly given.
>
> God help me to make good my vow, and God bless all of you who are willing to share in it.

Broadcasting on her 21st birthday, 21 April 1947.

Sixty-one years later, she said this in her 2008 Christmas broadcast:

I hope that, like me, you will be comforted by the example of Jesus of Nazareth who, often in circumstances of great adversity, managed to live an outgoing, unselfish and sacrificial life.

Countless millions of people around the world continue to celebrate his birthday at Christmas, inspired by his teaching.

He makes it clear that genuine human happiness and satisfaction lie more in giving than receiving; more in serving than in being served.

We can surely be grateful that, two thousand years after the birth of Jesus, so many of us are able to draw inspiration from his life and message, and to find in him a source of strength and courage.

Christmas 2008.

3 Ceremony & Sincerity

Elizabeth's Coronation was the most watched event in the history of television at the time.

So intense was the interest that more TV sets were bought in the two months before the Coronation than in any two month period since then. In fact, more than half the UK population, some 27 million people, watched it, gathering together in the homes of people with a set. A further 11 million people listened on the radio.

But the significance of the event is not that a lot of people watched it or enjoyed its grandeur. The significance lies not in the display of symbols and stunning robes. The significance lies in the Queen's understanding of what she was committing herself to do.

Every element of the service pointed in one direction: she was vowing to serve her people as a servant of God.

The Queen understood that her authority was not conferred by Parliament, nor inherited from her earthly father, but came from God, and it was to him that she would be ultimately accountable.

The words, symbols and rituals of the Coronation service were devised in AD 973. They were designed to highlight the values that monarchs should seek to uphold, the kind of person they should seek to be and the priorities of the heavenly King they would pledge themselves to serve.

The Royal Sceptre with its magnificent diamond-encrusted cross and what is believed to be the world's largest diamond, known as the Star of Africa.

Power

The Queen was given an orb with more than six hundred jewels and pearls, with a cross mounted on top to symbolise the rule of Jesus Christ over the earth. This symbol of power put into her hand indicates that she is the servant of a greater king, Christ, represented by the cross.

Wisdom

A single diamond in just one of the sceptres has an estimated value of £400 million, but the Moderator of the Church of Scotland presented the Queen with an object described in the service as 'the most valuable thing that this world affords'. It was the Bible.

For Christians, the Bible is the most valuable thing on earth because it is God's message to all humankind. It shows us what God is like. It reveals his love and commitment to us, what his Son has done for us, how we can know and enjoy him, and how we can live and love in his ways.

The Orb originally made for the Coronation of Charles II in 1661.

'The most valuable thing that this world affords.'

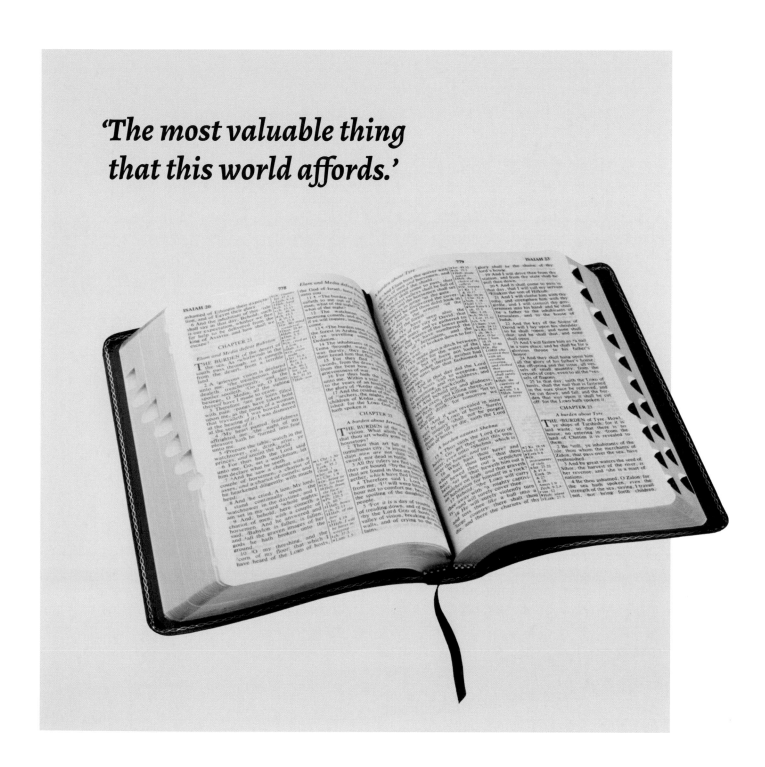

Mercy

There are a number of Coronation swords, reflecting the Queen's role in administering justice. Curiously, two of the swords have had the tip of their blades broken off. This is to remind monarchs that though they should exercise judgement they should also practise mercy, in line with the character of God. As the prophet Micah put it in the Bible:

> *What does the Lord require of you?*
> *To act justly and to love mercy and to*
> *walk humbly with your God.*

The importance of mercy was reinforced during the ceremony as the Queen held two sceptres. In her right hand, the sceptre with the cross, and in her left, the sceptre called the Rod of Equity and Mercy topped with a white enamelled dove, a symbol of God's Holy Spirit, resting on a gold orb with a cross on it, again symbolising the sovereign's spiritual role under God.

The Secret Ceremony

There was only one moment in the ceremony that was not televised. It was considered too sacred to show.

As Handel's anthem *Zadok the Priest* is sung, the symbols of the Queen's status are removed – the crimson velvet robe, the diamond diadem, the coronation necklace.

And then there she is, in a simple white dress.

She looks like a bride – young, beautiful, delicate – except that the dress is far less elaborate than her wedding gown. There is a ring, but there is no groom. Elizabeth is not giving herself to a husband but to a people.

At that point the Archbishop anoints her with holy oil and pours it onto her hands, her chest and her head to show she is being set apart to serve and love her people in all her actions, with all her heart and with all her mind.

The Sword of Mercy with its symbolically blunt tip.

Preparing for the anointing in Westminster Abbey, 2 June 1953.

In that commitment, she follows the example of Christ who was also anointed, as the word 'Christ' means, and set apart not to be served but to serve and, in his case, to sacrifice his life so we can have life that lasts forever.

Royal biographer William Shawcross wrote:

When Queen Elizabeth II was crowned in 1953, she found, like her mother before her, an almost sacrificial quality at the heart of the service... It was the moment when the holy oil was applied to her, rather than her crowning with St Edward's crown of solid gold, that was of supreme importance for the Queen. Indeed it was the most solemn and important moment of her entire life.

4 Working in Service

The Queen works hard. Very hard.

In fact, she has worked more than 50 hours a week for most of her working life and still works more than 40. In her 90th year.

She takes her role as Head of State seriously. Every day of the year, except for Christmas and Easter, she reads the red box of papers that are collated from the Prime Minister's office and other key government departments, including the security services. She is referred to as Reader No 1. Every week she meets the Prime Minister. She does not determine policy but she takes her constitutional right and duty to express her views on government matters very seriously – usually through the use of questions. No one has ever reported the content of these meetings but many of her Prime Ministers have stated publicly how helpful they have found them.

Apart from that, the Queen deals with hundreds of papers and pieces of correspondence every week. She also has a heavy schedule of visits. Whilst some are official State visits designed to develop goodwill and increase trade, many simply involve her going to quite ordinary places to celebrate good work of all kinds – in business, manufacturing, charities,

Top left: The Queen with Noidi Okereke Onyiwke, Director General of the Nigerian Stock Exchange, at the State House, Abuja, 3 December 2003.

Top right: The Queen presenting Mother Teresa of Calcutta with the Order of Merit, Delhi, November 1983.

Bottom: The Queen talks to a veteran at the 'Not Forgotten' Association Garden Party, Buckingham Palace, 6 June 2013.

senior citizens' care homes, youth development, music, the arts. She has an amazing ability to show genuine interest whoever she is with, wherever she goes.

The Queen works hard because she is committed to service.

And that comes from her commitment to follow the ways of Christ. At Christmas in 2012 she said:

> *This is the time of year when we remember that God sent his only Son 'to serve, not to be served'. He restored love and service to the centre of our lives in the person of Jesus Christ. It is my prayer this Christmas Day that his example and teaching will continue to bring people together to give the best of themselves in the service of others.*

> *My work, and the work of my family, takes us every week into that quiet sort of 'public life', where millions of people give their time, unpaid and usually unsung, to the community.*
>
> The Queen, 1998

The carol, 'In the Bleak Midwinter', ends by asking a question of all of us who know the Christmas story, of how God gave himself to us in humble service: 'What can I give him, poor as I am? If I were a shepherd, I would bring a lamb; if I were a wise man, I would do my part'. The carol gives the answer, 'Yet what I can I give him – give my heart'.

The Queen's work is an expression of her desire to serve others. She is not a hired servant who is required to do lots of tasks; she is a Queen who chooses to serve her people through doing the work that will best contribute to the nation's health.

Furthermore, just as she sees her own work as service so she sees other people's work in the same way. Indeed, though she meets lots of celebrities and

The Shooter & the Intruder

On almost every visit to any part of Britain, or indeed the world, the Queen walks about in a way that makes her a relatively easy target for an assassin. She has deliberately and courageously chosen a low level of security precisely so that she can engage with people. As Douglas Hurd, former Foreign Secretary, put it: *'The Queen has decided that in order to do her duty she must behave in ways that make her impossible to protect.'*

Furthermore, when danger comes, she is, by all accounts, unflappable. Famously, during the Trooping of the Colour in 1981, when the Queen rode side-saddle, unflanked by other riders, six shots rang out. Unperturbed, the Queen simply bent forward to pat her horse, Burmese, and carried on as if nothing had happened. The shots turned out to be blanks but the Queen did not know that.

Similarly, in 1982, an intruder, Michael Fagan, found his way into her Buckingham Palace bedroom. Afterwards when someone applauded the calm way she handled the situation, she said, *'You seem to forget that I spend most of my time conversing with complete strangers.'*

The Queen moments after a spectator fired six shots at her, 13 June 1981.

24

personally confers honours on more than 2,000 people a year who have in an extraordinary variety of ways contributed to our society, she is a constant champion of the ordinary citizen. In her Christmas broadcast of 1980 she said:

As I go about the country and abroad I meet many people who, all in their own ways, are making a real contribution to their community. I come across examples of unselfish service in all walks of life and in many unexpected places.

Some people choose their occupation so that they can spend their lives in the service of their fellow citizens.

We see doctors, nurses and hospital staff caring for the sick; those in the churches and religious communities; in central and local Government; in the armed services; in the police and in the courts and prisons; in industry and commerce.

It is the same urge to make a contribution which drives those seeking the highest standards in education or art, in music or architecture.

Others find ways to give service in their spare time, through voluntary organisations or simply on their own individual initiative contributing in a thousand ways to all that is best in our society.

It may be providing company for the old and housebound; help for the disabled; care for the deprived and those in trouble; concern for neighbours or encouragement for the young.

To all of you on this Christmas Day, whatever your conditions of work and life, easy or difficult; whether you feel that you are achieving something or whether you feel frustrated; I want to say a word of thanks.

And I include all those who don't realise that they deserve thanks and are content that what they do is unseen and unrewarded. The very act of living a decent and upright life is in itself a positive factor in maintaining civilised standards.

Work may be a way that we provide for ourselves but at its best it is also a way that we serve others, contribute to other people's wellbeing and help our nation flourish.

The Queen's inspiration for her view of her own work and others springs from

In your relationships with one another, have the same mindset as Christ Jesus: who, being in very nature God, did not consider equality with God something to be used to his own advantage; rather, he made himself nothing by taking the very nature of a servant...

Paul's letter to the church in Philippi, circa AD 62

Christ's own example of humble and sacrificial service. In 1986 she said:

His (Jesus') life thus began in humble surroundings, in fact in a stable, but he was to have a profound influence on the course of history, and on the lives of generations of his followers. You don't have to be rich or powerful in order to change things for the better and each of us in our own way can make a contribution.

The Queen did not choose her work, she inherited it. But she has chosen to do her work in a generous-hearted way, and has clearly found joy in serving, in following the example of the Son of God, the King who rules the Universe and yet was prepared to serve others and give his life that others might live.

The Prince & the Chauffeur

The Queen is by all accounts an accomplished mimic – many people have returned the favour, though rarely in her company – and that reflects a joyous sense of humour, and perhaps a certain mischievous streak.

Part of her job is to entertain State visitors. In 1998, Crown Prince Abdullah of Saudi Arabia was visiting the Queen at Balmoral. After lunch Her Majesty asked the Prince if he would like a tour of the estate. He agreed and, in due course, was guided to the front seat of a Land Rover, with his interpreter behind him.

In Saudi Arabia, the government prevents women from driving, so the Prince was perhaps unprepared to see the Queen getting into the driving seat next to him, setting off at speed along the narrow estate roads, and talking constantly. The ruffled Abdullah pleaded with the Queen through his interpreter to slow down and keep her eyes on the road. It is not clear that she took any notice.

She employs
1200
people...

...but feeds
her own **dogs**

5 Fezes, Football & Faith

The year is 1964 and the occasion is the Royal Variety Performance at the London Palladium.

The Queen is being introduced to the stars of the show. The uninhibited, and occasionally fez-wearing, comedian Tommy Cooper asks her if she minds answering a personal question.

'No,' she says, 'But I might not be able to give you a full answer.'
'Do you like football?' asks Cooper.
'Well, not really,' the Queen replies.
'In that case, do you mind if I have your Cup Final tickets?'

It's certainly not a question that anyone would bother asking her football-loving grandson William. Still, the Queen's answer is both clever and gracious. She is open to sharing something of herself so she doesn't immediately say 'No' to Tommy Cooper but at the same time she protects her privacy. As she put it, 'I might not be able to give you a full answer.'

There are a great many things which we don't know about the Queen. She met with Margaret Thatcher every week for 11 years but no one really knows what she thought of her. Or of Tony Blair. In an age when we are besieged by armies of celebrities telling us about almost every aspect of their lives in a variety of media, the Queen has kept most of her thoughts to herself. She may have a great many strongly held, well-considered personal opinions about a great many matters but we don't know what they are.

Curiously, that is not the case about her faith in Jesus.

About Jesus she has been remarkably, one might say, uncharacteristically open about what she believes.

And this is made most clear in her annual Christmas broadcasts where she speaks of Jesus Christ as 'an inspiration,' a 'role model' and 'an anchor' in her life; where she makes reference to the circumstances of his birth, to his death and to his resurrection. And for her, all of this is grounded in historical fact. In the millennial celebratory year she said:

Christmas is the traditional, if not the actual, birthday of a man who was destined to change the course of our history. And today we are celebrating the fact that Jesus Christ was born two thousand years ago; this is the true Millennium anniversary.

The simple facts of Jesus' life give us little clue as to the influence he was to have on the world. As a boy he learnt his father's trade as a carpenter. He then became a preacher, recruiting twelve supporters to help him. But his ministry only lasted a few years and he himself never wrote anything down. In his early thirties he was arrested, tortured and crucified with two criminals. His death might have been the end of the story, but then came the resurrection and with it the foundation of the Christian faith.

A wooden cross on St Cuthbert's Isle, Northumberland, named after the 7th century shepherd who became a monk, establishing Christianity in the north of England.

Even in our very material age the impact of Christ's life is all around us. If you want to see an expression of Christian faith you have only to look at our awe-inspiring cathedrals and abbeys, listen to their music, or look at their stained glass windows, their books and their pictures.

But the true measure of Christ's influence is not only in the lives of the saints but also in the good works quietly done by millions of men and women day in and day out throughout the centuries.

Many will have been inspired by Jesus' simple but powerful teaching: love God and love thy neighbour as thyself - in other words, treat others as you would like them to treat you. His great emphasis was to give spirituality a practical purpose.

Indeed, the measure of how Jesus Christ influences the Queen is not only in her public pronouncements but in the priorities she sets for her life and in the way she goes about her ordinary daily tasks.

She is extraordinarily respectful of other people. She is almost never late for anything or anyone, regardless of their rank. Though she knows others would wait, and perhaps would not be offended, she sees lateness as a mark of disrespect. The only time she was ever late for the Opening of Parliament was when she left her reading glasses behind in the Palace.

This deep respect for others manifests itself in how she treats her staff – they are never 'servants' to her – and she almost never calls any of her staff when they are off-duty in the evenings, at the weekend or on holiday.

She respects their privacy and their family life. Compare the Queen with the endless list of despotic rulers that litter history, or the many over-demanding bosses that sour our workplaces. By contrast, Elizabeth II shows us how power can be used considerately.

A Tale of Two Simes'

The Queen receives thousands of letters and cards but she has an amazing memory for detail and tremendous care for individual people.

Every year from 1952 Albert Alfred Simes sent a Christmas card from Izmir in Turkey to the reigning monarch until he died in 2011 aged 102. In 1972, he was invited to meet the Queen at a reception in Izmir. His grandson, Andrew, writing on Facebook, recalls the event:

'When it was his turn to be introduced to the Queen, instead of a formal handshake, she paused, smiled, and quipped: "So it's you who keeps sending me those lovely Christmas cards."'

When his grandfather died in the summer of 2011, Andrew took up the baton and sent a Christmas card to the Queen. The following January, he received a letter from her. Andrew explains:

'In it was written: "When I received a letter from a different Simes this Christmas, I instructed my office to research your grandfather's whereabouts. Therefore it is with much sadness, I have learned of his passing and extend my condolences to you and your family." I couldn't fight back the tears then, nor can I fight them back every time I remember this story of two people who left a lifelong impression on each other.'

6 Side Doors & Private Priorities

You can hear the car crunch to a halt from inside the old building.

The driver is reputedly rather firm on the brakes. A minute or so later a 5 foot 4 inch woman comes through the small side door and sits down in a pew. It is the Queen coming unannounced to join the local congregation of Sandringham Church for the Sunday service, as she often does when she is in residence on the Sandringham Estate. There's no chauffeur, no ceremony, no fuss. She often doesn't even sit in the special seat that only she can occupy but simply sits in one of the pews at the front. She comes in the side door because she doesn't want to draw attention to herself. But she does want to go to church. Not because she is expected to, not because she needs to be seen, but because she wants to be there.

Her trust in Jesus Christ is central to her.

And you can see it in so many ways. She doesn't *have* to invite a different church minister every weekend of her Balmoral holiday to spend time with her family but she does.

She doesn't *have* to go to church every week but she does.

And on the day of Princess Diana's death she didn't *have* to take her two grieving grandsons to their local church in Balmoral, but she did. In fact, some people criticised her for it. Still, in times of pressure, tragic loss, or death, if you are a believer in a living God, it is precisely to him and to fellow believers, that you turn for strength and comfort, perspective and prayer.

Similarly, she doesn't *have* to stage a children's Christmas party in the Buckingham Palace stables hoping it 'helps to bring the traditional story alive' but she does. She doesn't *have* to find out which children have won prizes at the Sandringham Estate Sunday school, then pay for and present the books to them, but she does.

And she does not actually *have* to mention Jesus in her Christmas addresses to the nation and the Commonwealth. It would be easy to reduce the birth of the incarnate Son of God to a gift-giving festival. But she does mention Jesus Christ.

And always as the climax of the broadcast.

Christians have the compelling example of the life and teaching of Christ and, for myself, I would like nothing more than that my grandchildren should hold dear his ideals which have helped and inspired so many previous generations.

The Queen, 1978

A rose from a well-wisher, as crowds gather to pay respects to Diana, Princess of Wales.

7 Christmas Presence

The tradition of Christmas broadcasts stretches back to 1932 and the Queen has been doing it almost every year since her accession to the throne.

Over the years, many topics recur – the importance of family, her concern for the lonely, for the poor, for the welfare of children, for the armed forces, and for the people of the Commonwealth. Similarly, there are themes she comes back to again and again, themes that are central to the way she follows the one whose birth Christmas celebrates. Two of the most frequent are forgiveness and loving your neighbour.

Forgiveness

In 2011 the Queen said,

Although we are capable of great acts of kindness, history teaches us that we sometimes need saving from ourselves – from our recklessness or our greed. God sent into the world a unique person – neither a philosopher nor a general (important though they are) – but a Saviour, with the power to forgive.

Forgiveness lies at the heart of the Christian faith. It can heal broken families, it can restore friendships and it can reconcile divided communities. It is in forgiveness that we feel the power of God's love.

And this is a conviction that the Queen has clearly tried to live out in her own life.

She has worked hard for peace and reconciliation all her life, particularly in her work to foster stronger relationships within the Commonwealth, in her work to heal divisions between Protestants and Catholics, and between the United Kingdom and Ireland. In this she has shown great courage and generosity of heart, especially as Prince Philip was brought up by Earl Mountbatten who was assassinated by the IRA. She made a successful State visit to the Republic of Ireland in 2011. The following year she made a two-day visit to Northern Ireland and met with people from both sides of the conflict, contributing significantly to the healing and reconciliation of the community. More broadly, the Queen was the first British monarch to meet the Pope since the Reformation.

Similarly, though it is very rare for monarchs to attend funerals of anyone other than royalty, close friends and relatives, she decided to attend the funeral of the Catholic Cardinal Basil Hume, despite the criticism she received for it.

At Christmas 1984 she said,

Above all, we must retain the child's readiness to forgive, with which we are all born and which it is all too

easy to lose as we grow older. Without it, divisions between families, communities and nations remain unbridgeable. We owe it to our children and grandchildren to live up to the standards of behaviour and tolerance which we are so eager to teach them.

It is particularly at Christmas, which marks the birth of the Prince of Peace, that we should work to heal old wounds and to abandon prejudice and suspicion.

What better way of making a start than by remembering what Christ said - "Except ye become as little children, ye shall not enter into the Kingdom of Heaven".

She returned to this theme in 2014, focusing on the source and inspiration for forgiveness:

For me, the life of Jesus Christ, the Prince of Peace, whose birth we celebrate today, is an inspiration and an anchor in my life. A role-model

*of reconciliation and forgiveness,
he stretched out his hands in love,
acceptance and healing. Christ's
example has taught me to seek
to respect and value all people of
whatever faith or none.*

Indeed, the Queen's strong faith in
Christ does not lead her to exclude
people of other faiths but rather to
embrace them, to accord them the
same respect and dignity she does
to those who share her beliefs.

Former Chief Rabbi Jonathan Sacks
met the Queen many times, and
recalls a moving occasion. He writes:

*Punctuality, said Louis XVIII of
France, is the politeness of kings.
Royalty arrives on time and leaves
on time. So it is with Her Majesty the
Queen, with one memorable exception.*

*The day was 27 January 2005, the
sixtieth anniversary of the liberation
of Auschwitz, and the place, St James'
Palace. The Queen was meeting a
group of Holocaust survivors.*

The Hands Across The Divide statue, Northern Ireland.

The gift I would most value next year is that reconciliation should be found wherever it is needed. A reconciliation which would bring peace and security to families and neighbours at present suffering and torn apart.

Remember that good spreads outwards and every little does help. Mighty things from small beginnings grow as indeed they grew from the small child of Bethlehem.

The Queen, 1976

When the time came for her to leave, she stayed. And stayed. One of her attendants said he had never known her to linger so long after her scheduled departure time. She gave each survivor – it was a large group – her focussed, unhurried attention. She stood with each until they had finished telling their personal story.

It was an act of kindness that almost had me in tears... It brought a kind of blessed closure into deeply lacerated lives.

We do not always appreciate the role the Queen has played in one of the most significant changes in the past sixty years: the transformation of Britain into a multi-ethnic, multi-faith society. No one does interfaith better than the Royal family, and it starts with the Queen herself.

Importantly, the Queen does not pretend that she believes that all religions are the same – she is a devoted Christian. Indeed, it is this combination of integrity and generous hospitality that makes her so popular among people of other faiths and none.

Rabbi Sacks puts it this way:

Jews have deep respect for the Queen and the royal family... Something similar, in my experience, is true of the other minority faiths in Britain. They value the Queen because they know she values them. She makes them feel, not strangers in a strange land, but respected citizens at home.

Her presence and her family's role as the human face of national identity is one of the great unifying forces in Britain, a unity we need all the more, the more diverse religiously and culturally we become.

Not surprisingly, as Supreme Governor of the Church of England, this is a role the Queen embraces. As she said in her address to the faith leaders of the United Kingdom at Lambeth Palace in 2012:

The concept of our established Church is occasionally misunderstood and, I believe, commonly under-appreciated. Its role is not to defend Anglicanism to the exclusion of other religions. Instead, the Church has a duty to protect the free practice of all faiths in this country.

It certainly provides an identity and spiritual dimension for its own many adherents. But also, gently and assuredly, the Church of England has created an environment for other faith communities and indeed people of no faith to live freely. Woven into the fabric of this country, the Church has helped to build a better society – more and more in active co-operation for the common good with those of other faiths.

And this is all part of her understanding of what it means to love your neighbour.

Top: The Queen lays small mirror tiles around the head of baby Jesus on a nativity collage made by schoolchildren at Southwark Cathedral, London, 7 December 2006.

Bottom left: On the Diamond Jubilee UK tour, the Queen visits Worcester, 11 July 2012.

Bottom right: Visiting the Sheikh Zayed Mosque, Abu Dhabi, November 2010.

Love your Neighbour

Caring for one's neighbour is a recurring theme in the Queen's broadcasts. Time and again she praises people who do, and calls on us all to look out for those around us. In 1975, commenting on the celebration of Christ's birth, she said of Jesus,

His simple message of love has been turning the world upside down ever since. He showed that what people are and what they do, does matter and does make all the difference.

He commanded us to love our neighbours as we love ourselves, but what exactly is meant by 'loving ourselves'? I believe it means trying to make the most of the abilities we have been given, it means caring for our talents. It is a matter of making the best of ourselves, not just doing the best for ourselves.

We are all different, but each of us has his own best to offer. The responsibility for the way we live life with all its challenges, sadness and joy is ours alone. If we do this well, it will also be good for our neighbours. If you throw a stone into a pool, the ripples go on spreading outwards.

A big stone can cause waves, but even the smallest pebble changes the whole pattern of the water. Our daily actions are like those ripples, each one makes a difference, even the smallest.

It does matter therefore what each individual does each day. Kindness, sympathy, resolution, and courteous behaviour are infectious. Acts of courage and self-sacrifice, like those of the people who refuse to be terrorised by kidnappers or hijackers, or who defuse bombs, are an inspiration to others.

And the combined effect can be enormous. If enough grains of sand are dropped into one side of a pair of scales they will, in the end, tip it against a lump of lead.

We may feel powerless alone but the joint efforts of individuals can defeat the evils of our time. Together they can create a stable, free and considerate society.

Given the Queen's frequent emphasis on our duty to others, it is no surprise that, apart from the accounts of Jesus' birth, the passage of the Bible she most often cites is Jesus' Parable of the Good Samaritan.

The Parable of the Good Samaritan

On one occasion an expert in the law stood up to test Jesus. "Teacher," he asked, "what must I do to inherit eternal life?"

"What is written in the Law?" he replied. "How do you read it?"

He answered, "'Love the Lord your God with all your heart and with all your soul and with all your strength and with all your mind'; and, 'Love your neighbour as yourself.'"

"You have answered correctly," Jesus replied. "Do this and you will live."

But he wanted to justify himself, so he asked Jesus, "And who is my neighbour?"

In reply Jesus said: "A man was going down from Jerusalem to Jericho, when he was attacked by robbers. They stripped him of his clothes, beat him and went away, leaving him half dead.

A priest happened to be going down the same road, and when he saw the man, he passed by on the other side. So too, a Levite, when he came to the place and saw him, passed by on the other side. But a Samaritan, as he travelled, came where the man was; and when he saw him, he took pity on him. He went to him and bandaged his wounds, pouring on oil and wine. Then he put the man on his own donkey, brought him to an inn and took care of him. The next day he took out two denarii and gave them to the innkeeper. 'Look after him,' he said, 'and when I return, I will reimburse you for any extra expense you may have.'

"Which of these three do you think was a neighbour to the man who fell into the hands of robbers?"

The expert in the law replied, "The one who had mercy on him."

Jesus told him, "Go and do likewise."

Luke 10: 25-37

The story of the Good Samaritan reminds us of our duty to our neighbour. We should try to follow Christ's clear instruction at the end of that story: 'Go and do thou likewise.'

The Queen, 1985

8 Strength for Adversity

What do you do when times are tough? Where do you turn?

The Queen has seen tough times. She saw her father take on a job he would rather not have done, grow ill under the strain of work and die young at 56. More recently she suffered the deaths of her mother and her sister in the same year.

Those events were made all the harder not only because she cared for them so very much but because family life has always been so important to the Queen, even though she has had to sacrifice much time with her family to serve the wider Commonwealth family. In 2007 she said:

> *In my experience, the positive value of a happy family is one of the factors of human existence that has not changed. The immediate family of grandparents, parents and children, together with their extended family, is still the core of a thriving community. When Prince Philip and I celebrated our Diamond Wedding last month, we were much aware of the affection and support of our own family as they gathered round us for the occasion.*
>
> *Now today, of course, marks the birth of Jesus Christ. Among other things, it is a reminder that it is the story of a family; but of a family in very distressed circumstances. Mary and*

Top left: The Queen with the Queen Mother and Princess Margaret.

Top right: The Duke and Duchess of Cambridge, walking to church with Prince George and Princess Charlotte.

Bottom: The Queen and Prince Philip with their children: Prince Charles, Prince Andrew, Princess Anne and Prince Edward.

Joseph found no room at the inn; they had to make do in a stable, and the new-born Jesus had to be laid in a manger. This was a family which had been shut out.

Perhaps it was because of this early experience that, throughout his ministry, Jesus of Nazareth reached out and made friends with people whom others ignored or despised. It was in this way that he proclaimed his belief that, in the end, we are all brothers and sisters in one human family.

But, as for so many of us, family life doesn't always go the way we would hope.

Famously, in November 1992, the Queen gave a speech at the Guildhall in the City of London:

1992 is not a year on which I shall look back with undiluted pleasure. In the words of one of my more sympathetic correspondents, it has turned out to be an 'Annus Horribilis'. I suspect that I am not alone in thinking it so. Indeed, I suspect that there are very few people or institutions unaffected by these last months of worldwide turmoil and uncertainty.

Despite being displaced and persecuted throughout his short life, Christ's unchanging message was not one of revenge or violence but simply that we should love one another.

The Queen, Christmas 2015

Here is the Queen at her understated best. Certainly, she would go on to mention the fire in Windsor Castle that had occurred only a few days before, but it was typical of her not to dwell on the detail of her own troubles but rather show sympathy for the challenges that others had faced.

The reality is that during that year Prince Andrew announced his separation from his wife; Princess Anne, divorced her husband; the Princess of Wales' biography *Diana, Her True Story* revealed the unhappiness of her marriage to Charles; Diana's affair with James Gilbey was confirmed in the press, as indeed was Charles' affair with Camilla. Apart from the terrible anguish of the sudden death or serious sickness of a child few of us are likely to experience such a high level of family distress in one year, and very few of us will ever have the added pressure of seeing it all made globally public.

The Queen's response was to express gratitude for the support of the prayers of others:

You, my Lord Mayor, and all those whose prayers - fervent, I hope, but not too frequent - have sustained me through all these years, are friends indeed. Prince Philip and I give you all, wherever you may be, our most humble thanks.

In a secular age, it is perhaps surprising to hear a leading international figure who is not a member of the clergy talk of prayer in the middle of a major public speech. The Queen didn't have to do so. She chose to do so. Perhaps simply because when times are tough, the knowledge that other people are praying to God on your behalf, is wonderfully heartening.

In 2013, she put it this way:

For Christians, as for all people of faith, reflection, meditation and prayer help us to renew ourselves in God's love, as we strive daily to become better people. The Christmas message shows us that this love is for everyone. There is no one beyond its reach.

Prayer – talking and listening to God – brings perspective and strength. Prayer leads to a renewed sense of God's love and care, to a renewed sense of security and worth.

And just as the Queen appreciates other people's prayers for her, so she prays for others, and for us. In 2011 she said:

In the last verse of this beautiful carol, O Little Town of Bethlehem, there's a prayer:

O Holy Child of Bethlehem, Descend to us we pray. Cast out our sin And enter in, Be born in us today.

It is my prayer that on this Christmas Day we might all find room in our lives for the message of the angels and for the love of God through Christ our Lord.

The Queen with one of her horses at the Royal Windsor Horse Show, May 2011.

9 Good Evening, Mr Bond

What kind of example do we expect our leaders or our bosses or our Queen to set?

In 1952, as the Archbishop of Canterbury, Geoffrey Fisher, helped the Queen prepare for her role, he told her that she was 'God-called to exert a spiritual power and lead her subjects by her personal example'.

Indeed, one of the most remarkable things about the Queen is her consistency of character. Despite unprecedented levels of relentless media scrutiny for her entire life, there has never been a whiff of scandal about the Queen herself.

Yes, she has worked hard, but she has also taken care to enjoy life, to pursue her enthusiasms, to spend time with family and friends. She has a strong and happy marriage to a man she clearly respects and whose company she enjoys.

Top: US President Barack Obama on a State visit to London, 24 May 2011.

Bottom left: Inspecting Prince Harry at his Passing Out Parade, Sandhurst, 12 April 2006.

Bottom right: The Queen and Prince Charles at the Braemar Highland Gathering, 1 September 2012.

She loves the countryside, her dogs and her horses. She still rides and is hugely respected by the racing community, and apparently adored by the Household Cavalry. World leaders say that there is something about her, a calm authority, a kind of peace perhaps, that marks her out. She takes her holidays and, though there are State papers to read every day, she takes no engagements. She doesn't justify her existence by how hard she works or feel that the world cannot get on without her. There is a time to rest.

> *God sent his only son 'to serve, not to be served'. He restored love and service to the centre of our lives in the person of Jesus Christ.*
>
> The Queen, 2012

In addition, she has shown herself to be enormously adaptable to changes in technology and culture, growing up before there was TV, the internet or jet engines. She has preserved the dignity of the role she has been asked to play but has known when to engage more informally. Indeed, she was 'delighted' to make her film debut in the 'Bond'-themed cameo at the opening of the 2012 Olympic Games. And though she does not particularly like football, as Tommy Cooper discovered, she does particularly enjoy watching marathons – not surprisingly perhaps. After all, she's been running one of her own for quite a long time now.

Certainly there is much more to Elizabeth than her faith in Christ but you cannot understand her without understanding her devotion to him. It shapes everything she does. As broadcaster Jeremy Paxman put it, her religious beliefs are 'quietly held', 'authentic and well-known'.

What kind of Queen might we have wished for?

The reality is that Elizabeth II has consistently, winsomely and publicly honoured the God she serves and has been an extraordinary example of joyful, persevering, life-affirming, generous-hearted, unstinting, wise service on behalf of others.

Six months before her Coronation, Elizabeth asked the people of the United Kingdom and Commonwealth to:

Pray that God may give me wisdom and strength to carry out the solemn promises I shall be making, and that I may faithfully serve Him and you, all the days of my life.

God, it is clear, has answered those prayers.

And we owe him and her enormous gratitude.

Happy birthday, your Majesty.

Working in over 200 countries, Bible Society is on a global mission to offer the Bible to every man, woman and child. This is because we believe that when people engage with the Scriptures, lives can be changed, for good.

HM The Queen is the Patron of Bible Society. Find out more about Bible Society's work at **biblesociety.org.uk**

The Queen's life of service and the way she talks openly about Jesus is inspiring. HOPE's goal is to see lives transformed in villages, towns and cities as Christians put their faith into words and action, serving their communities in Jesus' name.

HOPE is a catalyst bringing churches of all denominations together. Find out more at **hopetogether.org.uk**

The Queen's faith makes a noticeable difference to her everyday life. But how does trusting Jesus change the way *you* might work, shop, relate to friends, watch a movie, surf the web, help people in need?

Find out more about how LICC empowers individuals and churches for whole-life discipleship at **licc.org.uk** or **facebook.com/LICCltd**

Credits

Getty Images, Ian Britton, International Olympic Committee, Press Association Images, Rex Shutterstock.

Sherard Cowper-Coles, *Ever the Diplomat: Confessions of a Foreign Office Mandarin*, HarperPress, 2013.
Douglas Hurd, *Elizabeth II, The Steadfast*, Allen Lane, 2015.
Andrew Marr, *The Real Elizabeth: An Intimate Portrait of Queen Elizabeth II*, St Martin's Griffin, 2012.
Jeremy Paxman, *On Royalty*, Penguin, 2007.
Chief Rabbi Jonathan Sacks, 'The Queen is Defender of all Britain's Faiths', *The Times*, 31 May 2012.
William Shawcross, 'Into the Future', *Newsweek* special issue, Volume 1 Issue 2.

Authors
Mark Greene is the Executive Director of LICC.
Catherine Butcher is HOPE's Communications Director.

Designer
Claire Simmons-Clark, Bible Society.

With special thanks to Derek Beal, Roy Crowne, Tom Robson, Anna Watkin and Paul Woolley.

Produced by CPO.